This book belongs to

_____

By Mrs Natalie

Ding, Dong, Dung

Welcome to a wild and wonderful world where poop becomes the star of the show! In "Ding, Dong, Dung," young explorers are invited to embark on a fun and fact filled journey through the diverse landscapes of South Africa, where they'll discover the weird and interesting secrets hidden within animal dung – also known as poop. From the majestic lions prowling the savannah to the graceful giraffes grazing on acacia trees, each creature in South Africa leaves behind its own special gift—poop!
But far from being gross, poop is a treasure map of information waiting to be uncovered.

Scratch & SNIFF

What do you smell?

JUST KIDDING! I hope all you could smell was the paper.

YUK!
Did you really think I would make you smell poop?

Poop Facts

Many animals, including carnivores like lions and hyenas, as well as herbivores like zebra and elephants, use their poop to mark territory. By leaving their scent in different locations, they communicate with other members of their species about their presence, dominance, and territory status. This helps to avoid conflicts and establish boundaries without direct fights. Some roll in others poop and use it for camouflage like wild dogs, to cover their own scent.

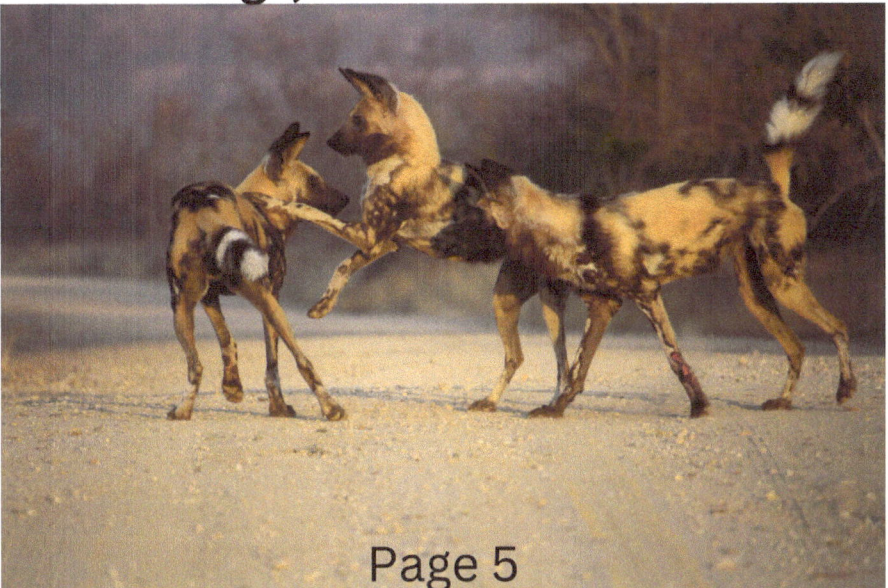

The importance of dung beetles

They help control the fly population.
They are harmless to humans.
They roll the balls with their back
feet, and when they finally get to
their place they call home, they then
dig a big hole and bury this big ball
of dung and then lay their eggs in it.
When the little beetles are born
then they eat the fungus and other
things that have grown in the ball.
They love elephant and rhino dung
as it is moist.

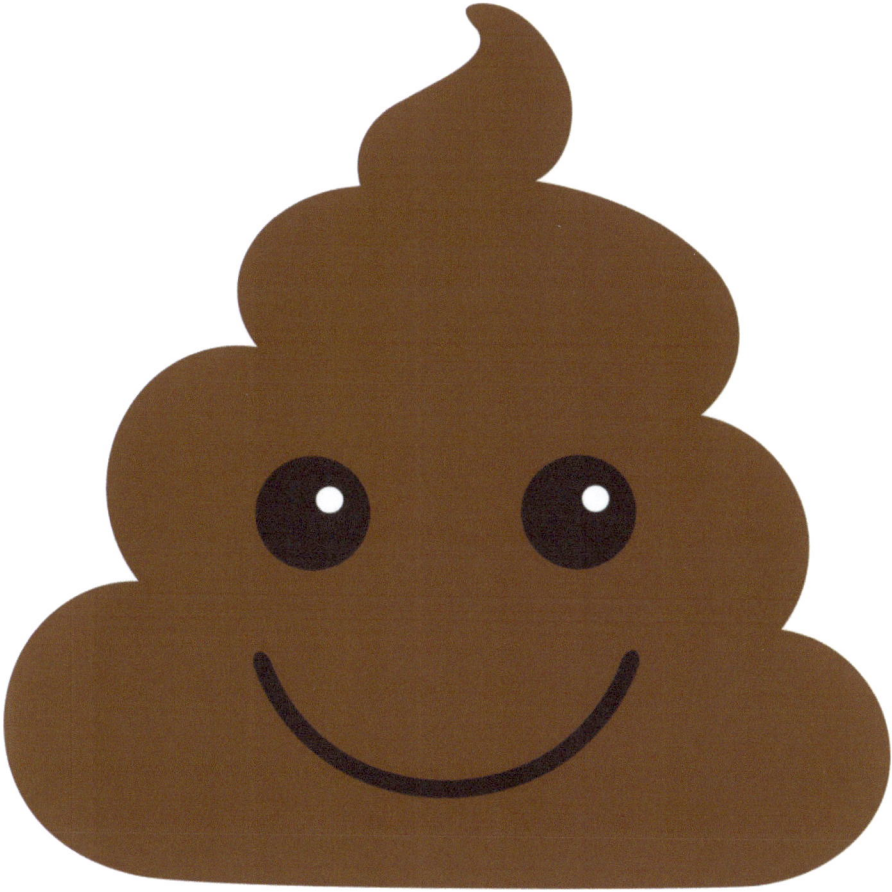

It is now time to find the animals and talk about their poop and dung.

DID YOU KNOW?

Poop from
rhinoceros is
called dung,
BUT....
Poop from a
baboon is not
called dung?
Find out later what
the poop from
baboons is called.

GIRAFFE

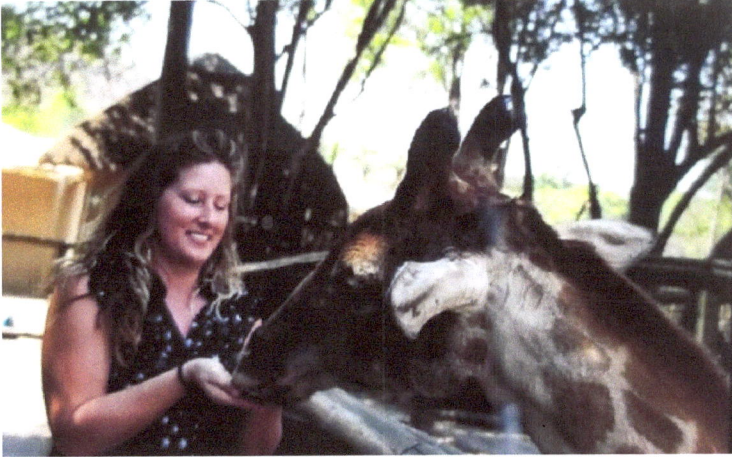

This tall animal can poop an amazing 15kg (33lbs) in 1 day!
Their poop is actually quite small for this large animal. They are identified as very small balls about the size of marbles.
They are similar to goats and camels and are ruminants which means every bit of nutrients are used from what they eat, so every bit of poop is waste.

Fun fact about the giraffe, is that they chew on random bones they find in the wild. This gives them calcium and nutrients. Cool right?
This giraffe I found chewing on the bones of a baboon skeleton. The baboon may have died
from natural causes or by a leopard attack.

My striped friends: ZEBRAS

Their poop contains special microbes that are tiny living cells that we cannot see with our eyes. These microbes live in the zebra stomach and help digest the plants it eats.
It can breakdown cellulose from cotton, twigs and newspaper, and someday may be used for more ecofriendly fuel.

FACT: A group of zebras is known as A DAZZLE

WHITE RHINOCEROS

Rhino dung in areas are called middens. These middens are specific areas the rhino bull chooses and uses the same spot to make big heaps.

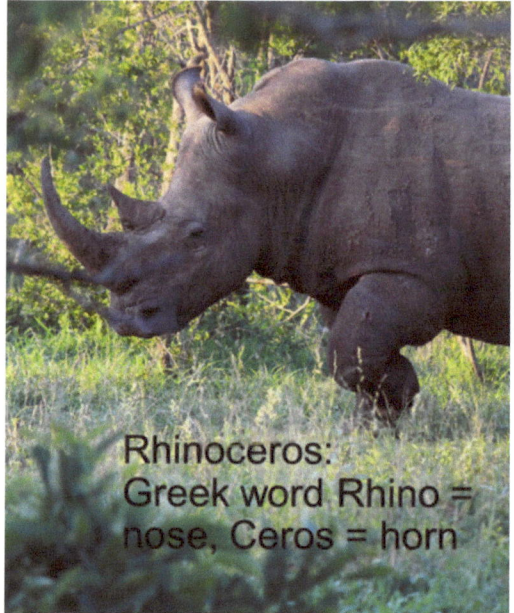

Rhinoceros:
Greek word Rhino = nose, Ceros = horn

To express their power, the males will poop in the middle of the midden and then kick it with their feet to spread the scent.
They can expel 50lb of dung per day. That is 22kg of dung. The dung beetles love the dung of rhino.

A group of rhinoceros is known as
A CRASH

We call them rhino for short

We can also use their dry dung to start a fire as well as putting some into a fire to keep away mosquitoes.

White rhino dung

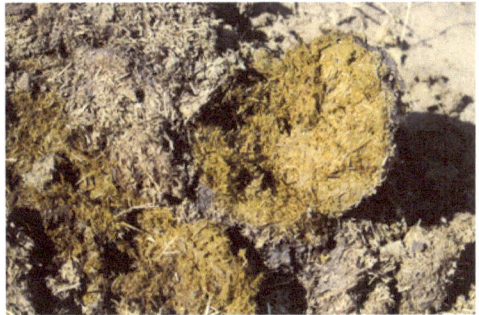

White rhino are grazers eating grass. This is their dung. When it dries over time, it blows away in the wind.

BLACK RHINO

They are browsers eating trees, and like the tamboti tree a lot. They chew off the twigs at a distinct 45 degree angle. Their dung is more brown, which is stained from the tannin chemical in the trees, and it contains sticks! The tamboti tree contains a poison to humans which can contaminate your food if you use it for a fire to cook your food. Stay away.

Sadly, I have not seen any black rhino in the wild to take a picture of, but I found their dung. They are rare and hide well.

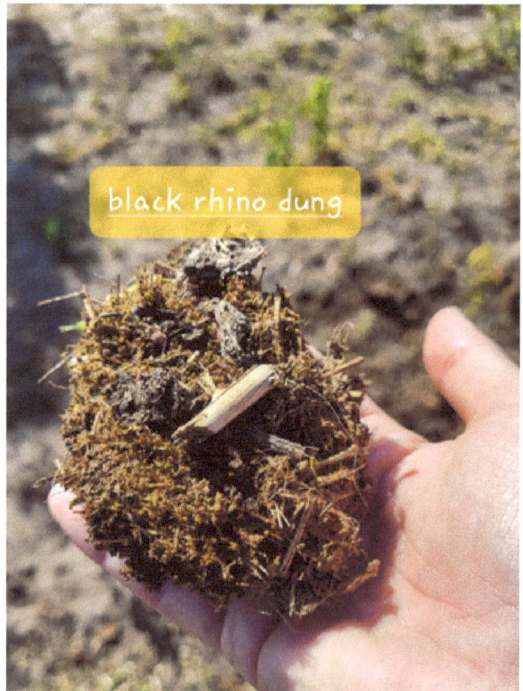

black rhino dung

ELEPHANTS

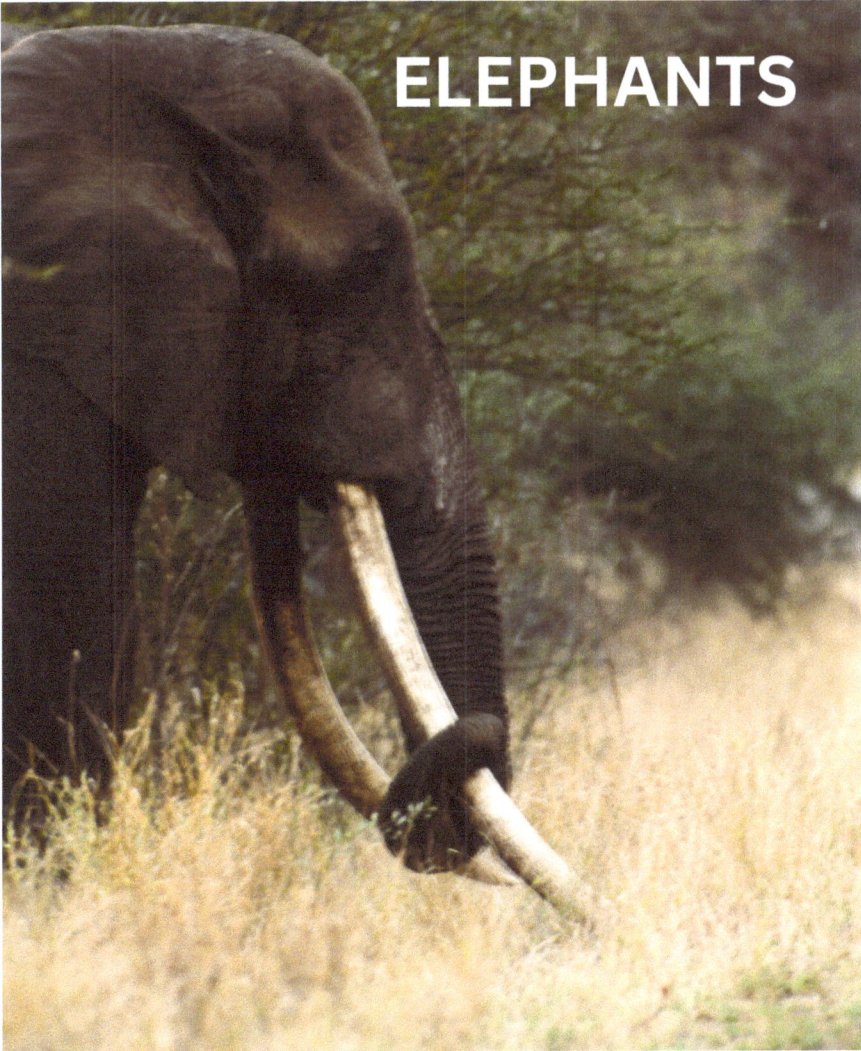

Elephants are the largest mammals on earth! So, it is no surprise that they poop the most, and largest in size too! Elephants poop up to 15 times in a day, producing about 113kg or 200lb of dung. Impressive isn't it!

elephant

This is just one piece of poop I am holding which is much larger than my hand! It is also quite heavy when it is fresh. It contains about 1/4 cup liquid. They only digest around 45% of what they eat.

The dried elephant dung can be lit on fire and used to keep bugs away.

Poop into paper... It can be washed, dried and turned into paper – about 115 sheets per day, from just one elephants' dung. You can easily buy the dung paper online.

Coffee time

In Thailand, elephants are helping to make coffee – yes, it is true. Elephants are helping to produce some of the rarest coffee in the world. They are being fed the coffee cherries, and then as they pass through their stomach, the protein is broken down and after about 72 hours they poop them out. Then they are washed and processed into a rare coffee that has hints of malt, spice, and hint of grass without the bitterness.
This coffee will cost you around 25$ per cup!
This can be found also online if you search elephant dung coffee.

SCAT

Lion poop or scat, can be quite distinctive. It is usually white in color once it dries from the digested calcium of eating bones. Hyena poop is similar in color.

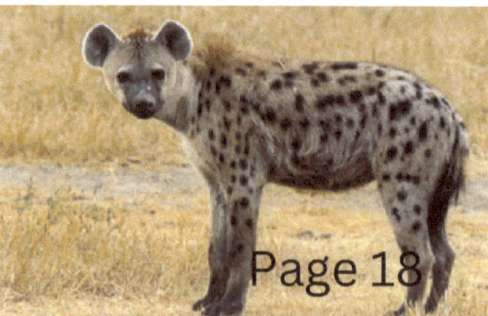

Tortoises actually eat the scat of hyena as it helps them have a strong shell from the calcium content.

HIPPOPOTAMUS

Poop rockets! They are messy poopers!
They will fling their dung with their
propeller tails and scatter it as far as
possible. They do this for a few reasons....
1.They do this to attract a mate
2.Scatter their scent
3.Mark their territory
They fling their dung on land which acts as
a fertilizer, as well as in the water and
plants and fish benefit from it.
They can poop a lot in one day. On land
they poop, and it also dries and eventually
blows away.

hippo scattered dung

This can look similar to a
rhino midden, but usually they
kick it into the road.
It dries very quickly.
They come out of the water at night
to eat grass and plants.
When it comes morning time again,
they head back to the water.

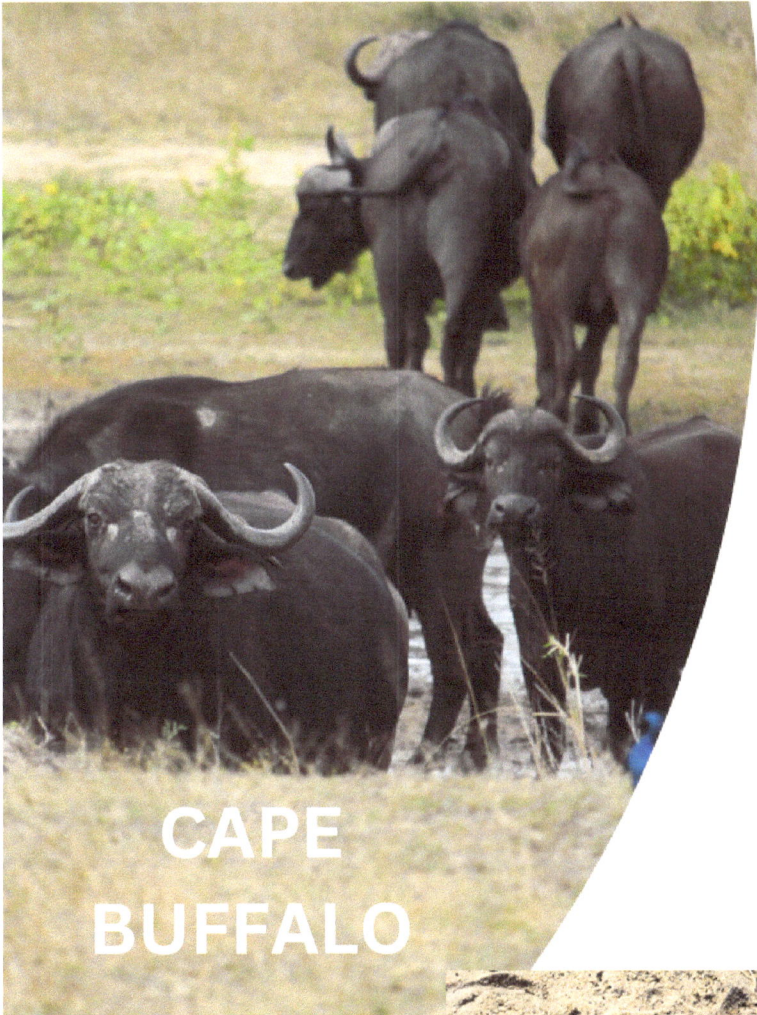

CAPE BUFFALO

Buffalo are bovine, so they make patties similar to cows.
IF you step in it, it will stick to your shoes!
Yuk.

buffalo

IMPALA

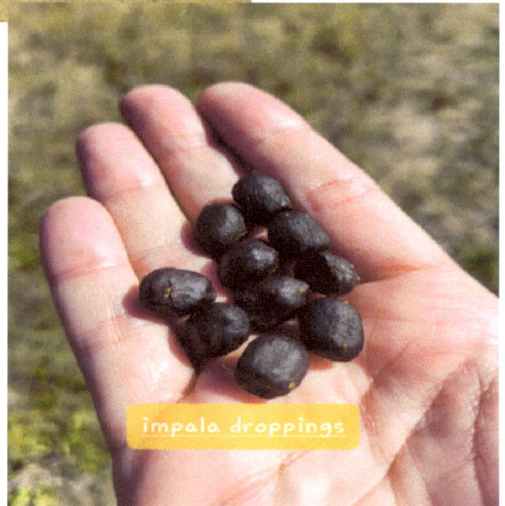

impala droppings

Impala are antelope that are very common in South Africa. They are usually found in large groups. They also make middens or large poop piles. Their poop is very small round balls.
It is not sticky, and it does not smell.

Blue wildebeest are funny looking animals. They are also very common around South Africa. This is what their poop looks like. It is a bit sticky and clumps together, so I did not pick any up.

wildebeest

NOW YOU
KNOW

What animal poop looks like, and some uses for it.

Poop terminology:

<u>Dung</u> refers to droppings of herbivores. (elephant, rhino, etc)
The droppings of carnivores (lions, hyena, etc) is called <u>scat</u>, and the droppings of omnivores is referred to as <u>feces</u> (baboons, humans, etc)

I am an Online Teacher

You can find me:
On OutSchool
Mrs Natalie Chiasson Weyers

Or email
mrsnatalie@travelteacher.ca

I have classes available:
- ESL
- Reading & Writing
- Classes about animals
~ and more

I have written many other
books, journals, etc, and you can find me
on amazon:
Search Mrs Natalie Chiasson

www.ingramcontent.com/pod-product-compliance
Lightning Source LLC
LaVergne TN
LVHW010030070426
835511LV00004B/101